The information provided herein is intended to be used for general information and is not provided as legal or other professional advice or as a legal service. If legal or other advice is required, services of an attorney should be sought.

IEP & SECTION 504 TEAM MEETINGS

...AND THE LAW

Thank you for the important work you do!

Together—moving from confusion to confidence, to get back to the mission of educating ALL children.

IEP & SECTION 504 TEAM MEETINGS

...AND THE LAW

MIRIAM KURTZIG FREEDMAN

CORWIN

A SAGE Publishing Company

FOR INFORMATION:

Corwin

A SAGE Company

2455 Teller Road

Thousand Oaks, California 91320

(800) 233-9936

www.corwin.com

SAGE Publications Ltd.

1 Oliver's Yard

55 City Road

London EC1Y 1SP

United Kingdom

SAGE Publications India Pvt. Ltd.

B 1/I 1 Mohan Cooperative Industrial Area

Mathura Road, New Delhi 110 044

India

SAGE Publications Asia-Pacific Pte. Ltd.

18 Cross Street #10-10/11/12

China Square Central

Singapore 048423

Publisher: Jessica Allan

Senior Content Development Editor: Lucas Schleicher

Associate Content Development Editor: Mia Rodriguez

Production Editor: Rebecca Lee

Typesetter: C&M Digitals (P) Ltd.

Proofreader: Sarah Duffy

Cover/Graphic Designer: Gail Buschman

Marketing Manager: Deena Meyer

MIX

Paper from
responsible sources
FSC® C103567

20 21 22 23 24 10 9 8 7 6 5 4 3 2 1

Contents

About the Author viii

Author's Acknowledgments xi

Preface xii

Introduction: You're kidding! Another law book for
educators and parents! 1

What is the purpose of an IEP team meeting? 7

What is the purpose of a 504 team meeting? 24

10 similarities between IEP and 504 team meetings 26

Differences between IEP and 504 meetings 52

IEP team meetings: Who, when, where, why, how 53

Section 504 team meetings 81

Good practices for both types of meetings 90

...Continued

Glossary 101

Additional Resources. 103

References and Cases 104

Visit the companion website at
http://resources.corwin.com/IEPandSection504
for downloadable resources.

About the Author

Miriam Kurtzig Freedman, JD, MA

Passionate about helping our public schools be excellent for ALL students, attorney Miriam Kurtzig Freedman works with people who want better schools and helps practitioners move from confusion to **confidence** when dealing with legal requirements. Why? So they can get back to the all-important mission of education!

Miriam has authored eight books and contributed articles to *The Wall Street Journal*, *Education Week*, *Education Next*, the *Journal of Law and Education*, and the *University of Chicago Law Review Online*, among other publications. She also contributes to *Medium.com*.

A school attorney, Miriam is of counsel to the Boston law firm of Stoneman, Chandler & Miller LLC. She provides clients and national

audiences with lively and practical keynotes, training, and consultation—all in "plain English"! A former teacher, Miriam "gets it"—what school folks need to know and do.

Miriam co-founded the annual Special Education Day (December 2) to both celebrate the success of special education and spur reform (**info@specialeducationday.com**). Among its reforms is SpedEx, the successful, voluntary, trust-building, child-centered dispute resolution model. A summary of her writing, speaking, and consulting is available at **www.schoollawpro.com**.

She received her law degree from New York University, master's from The State University of New York at Stony Brook, and bachelor of arts from Barnard College (Columbia University). When not engaged in public education activities, Miriam loves to hang out at the café and spend time with her family, especially her granddaughter!

Contact Information

If you are interested in Miriam's books, articles, or presentations (including keynotes, workshops, and consultation), or if you have questions/comments about this book, please visit **www.schoollawpro.com** and contact Miriam at **Miriam@schoollawpro.com**.

Issues of interest include:

- Building Special Education 2.0 for the 21st century!
- Trust-based special education
- Grading, reporting, and graduating students under state and federal laws
- . . . and whatever else is relevant to promote real learning in our schools!

Schools, the law, and common sense!

Author's Acknowledgments

Many, many people encouraged me along the way and I'm most grateful.

Steve Sandoval and Nate Levenson continue to inspire my reform efforts with their vision and practice in creating excellence in schools. I'm grateful to colleagues for reviewing this manuscript and for their insights and updates—Andrea Bell Bergeron, Mary Bevernick, and Anne Delfosse.

Two informal reform groups—the All-in-Network and the Unique Forum—are a source of inspiration and out-of-the-box thinking for which I am grateful. My "second family," my law firm, Stoneman, Chandler & Miller, continues to be a source of friendship and excellence.

Finally, my wonderful family and friends—who encourage my work. Together, let's make schools work for everyone!

The opinions and any errors are mine.

Preface

Thank you! Back in 2008, you—my colleagues, clients, and audiences across the nation—asked for this little flipbook of law to clarify confusion about these laws. I'm grateful for the wonderful stories, insight, and hopes we've shared—as we work together for better schools for ALL students (general and special education).

It's been my passion for years—as a teacher, hearing officer, and school attorney—to do what I can to help ensure that students have the opportunity to learn what they need to learn. **Why the passion?** Perhaps because I owe so much to my wonderful public schools and teachers in Flemington, New Jersey, from when I immigrated to America in the fourth grade. Now I want to spread the legal knowledge so children today also have wonderful opportunities.

Before going further, let's remember: parent satisfaction surveys show that most parents are *satisfied* or *very satisfied* with the special education services their children receive. Yet special education still fosters many costly and damaging disputes. This book is designed to ease them—so everyone can get back to the vital mission of teaching and learning for all students!

Now, after three revisions and updates, I'm proud to partner with Corwin to expand the reach of this vital information, first written in 2008. I'm struck by the fact that the basics remain. It's still

about providing students with disabilities educational benefits and fostering progress in the context of helping ALL students thrive. It's still about building trust among teachers, students, and parents.

This little flipbook of law is a companion to *Grading, Reporting, Graduating...and the Law*. They both bridge the gap between the worlds of law and education—in plain English so schools can protect individual rights and provide excellent education for ALL students.

Introduction: You're kidding! Another law book for educators and parents!

We've had enough!

But wait! *IEP and Section 504 Team Meetings...and the Law* is different. It's quick. It's fun. It's a flipbook of law that bridges the gap between educators (and parents) and lawyers. It answers the following important question:

> **What do educators and parents need to know and do to conduct meetings that are legal and efficient, build positive and trusting relationships, and get the job done?[1]**

This little flipbook of law is an antidote for the complexity surrounding these issues. We need to clarify requirements—so educators can get back to their classrooms, parents can get back to being parents, and, most important, students can get back to learning.

---

[1]These meetings have different names in different states. Here, the term "team meeting" is used for both IEP and Section 504 meetings. Note that IEP meetings have different names in different states. Additionally, a Section 504 meeting may be called a "Section 504 group meeting," a "504 group meeting," a "504 plan meeting," "a 504 meeting," etc. Check your local practice.

1

...Continued

This little flipbook of law includes reference to the 2004 *Individuals with Disabilities Education Act* (hereinafter, the IDEA), and 2006, 2008, 2016, and 2017 amendments to Part B (of the IDEA) regulations; Section 504 of the *Rehabilitation Act of 1973* (Section 504, or simply 504) and its regulations; the 2009 *Amendments Act of the Americans with Disabilities Act* (ADAAA) and its 2010 and 2016 further amendments; the 2015 *Every Student Succeeds Act* (ESSA), which replaced the *No Child Left Behind Act* (NCLB)—both of which are reauthorizations of the 1965 *Elementary and Secondary Education Act* (ESEA); the Supreme Court's 2017 *Endrew F. v. Douglas County School District RE-1* and 1982 *Board of Education of Hendrick Hudson Central School District v. Rowley* (hereinafter *Endrew F.* and *Rowley*) decisions,[2] selected due process and other court decisions, and U.S. Department of Education guidance.

Phew, that's a mouthful! Not to worry. We'll work to make sense of it!

---

[2] A word about case and document names in this little flipbook of laws. The full names, citations, and years of court and hearing officer decisions—as well as ED guidance—are spelled out the first time they appear. Thereafter, names may be abbreviated and citations omitted. References and Cases lists complete citations for all decisions.

What is the difference between an IEP team meeting and a Section 504 meeting?

Before we get to the law, let's ask these basic questions:

Why have meetings? I always like to start with and recommend Simon Sinek's book *Start With Why* and his many TED talks.

What purpose(s) do they serve? And not serve?

School personnel need to understand what team meetings are and what they are NOT, and how to steer these meetings aright when they go off course.

Ready? Almost!

One final thought before we start. Let's not get overwhelmed. Here, we deal with legal requirements only—not politics, education, or the latest trends. We learn what schools *have* to do—not whether the laws or regulations are good or recommended. We leave those discussions for another day.

Figure 1 Circles of influence

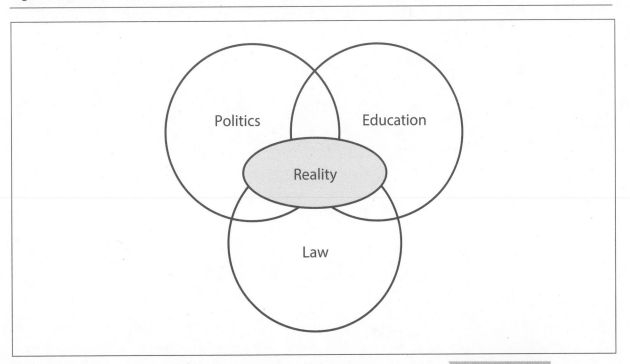

Let's start with the basics. Recall that the special education law, the IDEA, and the anti-discrimination law, Section 504—each have different purposes.[3]

The **IDEA** requires schools to develop Individualized Education Programs (IEPs) for eligible students[4] with disabilities so they can receive a free appropriate public education (FAPE). Let's quickly review the two important Supreme Court decisions mentioned above about a FAPE.

In 2017, in *Endrew F.*, the Court held that IEPs are to "be reasonably calculated to enable the child to make progress appropriate in light of the child's circumstances."

In 1982, in *Rowley*, the Court held that IEPs should be "reasonably calculated to enable the child to receive educational benefits." The 2017 decision generally followed and is consistent with the Court's earlier decision. *Endrew F.* also highlighted the reality that there are two groups of students with disabilities. Thus, *Rowley* dealt with a student working at grade level while *Endrew F.* dealt with a student who was not. The Court held that IEP goals for all students with disabilities should have "challenging objectives" and be "appropriately ambitious."

---

[3]Please see list of acronyms in the back of this little flipbook of laws.

[4]The words "child/children" and "student/students" are used interchangeably herein.

Section 504 does *not* require educational *benefits* or *progress* for the child. Instead, it is an anti-discrimination law that requires schools to provide eligible students with disabilities the same opportunities as their **average** nondisabled peers have. Over the years, schools have come to develop written "504 plans" to document the services and accommodations they provide. Recall that while writing a 504 plan is not legally mandated, it's often considered to be a best practice.

Remember the adage, *"If it's not in writing . . . it didn't happen."*

In the **ADAAA,** which became effective in 2009, Congress expanded the definition of "disability." The OCR (Office for Civil Rights) is the federal agency that enforces Section 504 and the ADAAA. You'll see many OCR letters and decisions in this little flipbook of laws.

First, let's focus on special education and IEPs. IEPs are developed at meetings called "IEP team meetings." More on these meetings next!

6

What is the purpose of an IEP team meeting?

It provides rights to both the student and parents through the IDEA's two prongs of rights—for students and for parents.

For the student, the IEP team's job is to (a) develop an IEP that provides a FAPE according to both *Endrew F.* and *Rowley*, as described above. The first prong.

For the parents, the IEP team provides them the opportunity to participate meaningfully in the development of the IEP (more on this later). The second prong.

But what is a FAPE?

Let's look at the letters—F. A. P. E. What does each stand for?

F—Free to the parents.

A—Appropriate; providing a program that is reasonably calculated (by the IEP team) to help the child make **progress** (*Endrew F.*) and receive **educational benefits** (*Rowley*).

P—Public; under public control, even if services are in a private setting.

E—Education.

More about the letters A and E!

A is for "appropriate." But what is "appropriate"? Good question! It's been debated for more than forty years! It's been subject to many interpretations, so that it can be seen as the "the full-employment for attorneys' term"!

Again, see the two Supreme Court decisions. Under *Rowley* (1982) the IEP needs to be "reasonably calculated to enable the child to receive educational **benefits**." Under *Endrew F.* (2017), the IEP needs to be "reasonably calculated to enable a child to **make progress** appropriate in light of the child's circumstances."

The IDEA provides a "basic floor of opportunity" for students with disabilities. How much progress or benefit should a FAPE provide? Courts use different adjectives to answer this question, such as *meaningful, measurable,* or *some* benefit. The benefit needs to be more than trivial or *de minimis*, but schools are not required to "maximize the potential of each handicapped child" or provide the best program for the child. As you can see, these words leave much room for debate—and the courts have been busy interpreting them since the law was enacted in 1975.

Further, a FAPE should be provided in the least restrictive environment (LRE) to the maximum extent **appropriate**. (Notably, not to the maximum extent **possible**, as it is often misquoted!) A world of difference here! Again, we've seen much court action on these terms over the years.

...Continued

IEPs need to include the child's "present levels of academic achievement and functional performance" and appropriate "measurable" goals to demonstrate (show, prove) progress.

In addition, the Supreme Court, in both of these decisions, has been very clear: the law does not guarantee any particular level of education and "cannot and does not" promise any particular educational outcome.

Lots to chew on here!

Here are examples of circuit court decisions about a FAPE.[5]

The term "measurable benefit" was first used by the First Circuit Court. In *C.D. v. Natick Public School District* (2019), the Court found that the student received a FAPE, despite the parents' argument that the repetition of goals from year to year indicated otherwise. See also *Roland M. v. Concord School Committee* (1990).

The Sixth Circuit famously used the car analogy. IEPs are to provide students with a "serviceable Chevrolet," not a "Cadillac." See *Doe v. Board of Education of the Tullahoma City Schools* (1993).

The "Chevy" must run well. It can't be a "lemon." It need not be a "Cadillac!"

---

[5]The United States is divided into eleven Circuit Courts of Appeals, which hear appeals from lower courts, such as district courts. Their decisions may be appealed to the Supreme Court. See Circuit Courts map on page 14.

11

Next we can ask...

Does a child's slow progress and the repetition of similar goals on an IEP from year to year mean that there's a denial of a FAPE? Not, according to *Endrew F.*, if the slow rate of progress is "appropriate in light of the child's circumstances." See *C.D. v. Natick* above.

Besides the above First Circuit decision, the Second and Third Circuits also have found that not to be a denial of a FAPE. See *F.L. v. Board of Education of the Great Neck Union Free School District* (2nd Cir. 2018)—hereinafter, *F.L. v. Great Neck*—and *K.D. v. Downingtown Area School District* (3rd Cir. 2018).

> **Bottom Line:** IEP teams should develop goals that are ambitious in light of the child's circumstances—even when they are not at grade level.

E is for "education." But what is "education"?

The IDEA speaks about "academic achievement and functional performance" in many places; for example, 20 USC Sec. 1414 (d)(1)(A). Look to state laws to define "education" and "educational performance."

Some states define education broadly—to include academic, emotional, social, behavioral, and physical needs. See, for example, *Mr. I. v. Maine School Administrative District No. 55* (1st Cir. 2007). The Court found that "educational performance" is more than academics. The student with Asperger's disorder—now considered part of the autism spectrum under *DSM-V*—generally had strong grades, but had difficulty in "communication," an area of educational performance listed in Maine's law, which made her eligible for special education services.

Other states focus on academics—the 3 R's, science, social studies, and so on. See, for example, *Hood v. Encinitas Union School District* (9th Cir. 2007). The parents' reimbursement claim for private school placement was denied because a student with a specific learning disability is not eligible for special education services. Prior to her removal from public school, the student consistently received average or above-average grades, even though she had an impairment. She did not need special education to learn in school.

The U.S. Office for Special Education Programs (OSEP) has chimed in in *Letter to Clarke* (OSEP 2007). OSEP writes, "It remains the Department's position that the term 'educational performance' as used in the IDEA and its implementing regulations is not limited to academic performance."

Practice Hint: Check court decisions in your state, your Circuit Court of Appeals, and your state laws and regulations.

13

Figure 2 Geographic boundaries of U.S. Courts of Appeals and U.S. District Courts

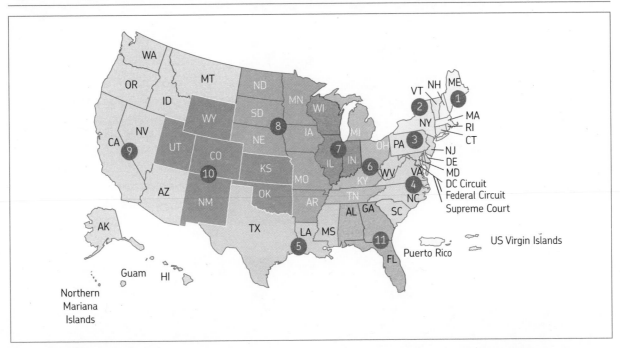

Source: https://www.uscourts.gov/

14

Let's discuss the "appropriate" standard a bit more.

Among issues that may arise at IEP meetings are these:

An argument may be made that the IEP is not appropriate because the gaps are not closing. Hmmm. . . . to untangle that argument, let's first clarify which **gap** we're talking about. There are two possible gaps.

The first gap is between the student's current performance and their[6] "circumstances," which we generally assume includes the student's potential.

The second gap is between the student and their age-level peers. Parents may argue that the gap between the student and their peers is widening (not narrowing) and therefore the IEP is not appropriate.

As for the first gap, yes, IEPs should work to close that. *Endrew F.* highlights the need for IEP goals to be "appropriately ambitious" and "challenging" so the student can make progress in light of their circumstances. But as for the second gap, the IDEA does not require that IEPs close it.

---

[6]See Merriam-Webster's Word of the Year 2019 explanation for updated language around use of the singular "they" pronoun when referring to one person of unspecified gender.

Courts have been unsympathetic to that argument.

See *E.R. v. Spring Branch Independent School District* (5th Cir. 2018), where a fourth grader's IEP that did not reflect the state's grade-level achievement standards was upheld, as it included "appropriately ambitious" goals in light of the child's circumstances.

And see *K.D. v. Downingtown* (2018) (cited above), where advancement at grade level was not required for all (or even most) students with disabilities.

See, again, *F.L. v. Great Neck* (2018), where the child was making slow progress that was **appropriate—even though slower than the parent preferred**.

Practice Hint: The purpose of an IEP is to help the child progress in light of their circumstances—it is not to pass state tests, close gaps with peers, "be successful," etc.

And a few more bullets to keep in mind.

- For all students, the ESSA requires schools to provide "evidence-based" instruction and interventions that have "evidence to support their effectiveness in improving student outcomes" and in meeting "challenging academic standards" (Section 1111, state plans (20 USC 6311)(b)(1); see also Section 8101 (21)).

- In special education, the basic premise is that schools choose the methodology they will use to educate the child.

- A team member, such as a parent, advocate, or outside evaluator, may argue for a different methodology than the one that school personnel proposed. However, as stated above, it is long established that schools have authority to select the methodology, so long as it provides a FAPE and, according to ESSA, is, when possible, "evidence-based."

  - Indeed, *Endrew F.* states that IEPs need not list a specific methodology! See *Questions and Answers on Endrew F. v. Douglas County School District Re-1* (ED 2017).

  - And see *R.Z.C. v. North Shore School District* (9th Cir. 2018, unpublished), where the district was not bound by the conclusions and recommendations of an independent evaluator. See also earlier similar cases *T.B. v. Warwick School Committee, et al.* (1st Cir. 2004) and *Grim v. Rhinebeck Central School District* (2nd Cir. 2003).

◼ A team member may argue that because a student got an F grade, they were denied a FAPE. Not so fast, here. Instead, the team needs to consider why that happened. Was it the student's lack of effort/failure to do work? Was it the school's failure to provide services? See *Edinburg (TX) Consolidated Independent School District* (OCR 2007) for a finding that the failure was due to the student's lack of effort.

Practice Hint: IEPs are not about student success or passing grades. They are about student learning! Students with IEPs or 504 plans have the same opportunity to succeed or fail as do all other students. In these types of situations—especially if a student is not progressing or there is another unexpected changed circumstance—the team should reconvene to consider what's going on!

IDEA eligibility determinations: Who needs an IEP?

Eligibility and "child find" issues generally go beyond the scope of this little flipbook of law. Additionally, both the IDEA and 504 have regulations about eligibility and evaluations for "English learners" (the term used in ESSA), who have also been described as "limited English proficient" students (the term used in the IDEA).

Child find, a "hot" area of litigation, is an affirmative duty that appears in the IDEA (20 USC 1412 (a)(3); 34 CFR 300.300-301). It requires schools to identify, locate, and evaluate all children with disabilities who reside in the district regardless of the severity of their needs.

While child find does not appear in the 504 law, the OCR has incorporated it into practice. The affirmative duty is triggered when the district has reason to suspect that a child who resides in the district has an impairment that may substantially limit the student in a major life activity. See discussion further on in the book.

Though all of these issues go beyond the scope of this little flipbook of law, it may be helpful to cite some recent cases—when eligibility was not found, and when it was.

IEP NOT REQUIRED—Sample cases

A student with an impairment is eligible for special education services only if they have an educational need. See *D.L. v. Clear Creek Independent School District* (5th Cir. 2017), where a high schooler with anxiety, depression, and attention deficit hyperactivity disorder (ADHD) did not require special education or related services under the IDEA.

And see *Durbrow v. Cobb County School District* (11th Cir. 2018), where the Eleventh Circuit found that a high schooler's ADHD did not impede his performance during his first three years in a program for high-achieving students. Thus, he did not establish a need for special education.

See also *Alvin Independent School District v. A.D.* (5th Cir. 2007), *Hood v. Encinitas* (9th Cir. 2007), and *Lincoln-Sudbury Regional Regional School District* (D. Mass. 2018), where parents sought special education for a high school student who was taking rigorous courses and suffered a concussion during field hockey practice. The Court found the student not eligible. The Court also found that the parents had brought the suit for "patently frivolous and unreasonable" reasons, leading the district to seek (successfully) recovery of its attorney fees.

IEP WAS REQUIRED—Sample cases

In *Board of Education of Montgomery County v. S.G.* (4th Cir. 2007), special education eligibility was found for a fifteen-year-old with schizophrenia because her emotional disturbance adversely impacted her educational performance so that the special education and related services were **necessary** for the student to receive an educational benefit from the educational program. The Board was ordered to fund her private therapeutic school. See also *Marshall Joint School District No. 2 v. C.D.* (7th Cir. 2010) and the First Circuit decision discussed earlier, *Mr. I. v. Maine School Administrative District No. 55* (2007).

Practice Hint: School personnel need to understand the legal requirements and acquaint themselves with trends. These include "red flags" that may lead to a child find referral, such as excessive absences and other attendance issues, truancy, student health issues, student behavior, and discipline.

When a school district (Local Education Agency, or LEA) finds a student not eligible for IDEA services, it may wish to consider eligibility for Section 504 services. Each situation is different.

See *Vance County (NC) Schools* (OCR 2009), where the OCR faulted the LEA for focusing narrowly on the student's academics without considering other needs, such as emotional or behavioral, triggering the need to consider the student's eligibility for a 504 plan.

Parent Rights

Besides ESSA's "parental and family engagement policy" (Title 1, Part A, Section 1116) for ALL parents, parents of students covered by the IDEA have the specific right to participate meaningfully in the development of the IEP for their child. The 1982 classic, *Rowley,* and the more recent (2017) *Endrew F.* highlight the fact that the IEP team has to comply with legal procedures, including providing parents with an opportunity to participate in the development of the IEP for their child. As stated in *Rowley:*

> *It seems to us no exaggeration to say that Congress placed every bit as much emphasis upon compliance with procedures giving parents and guardians a large measure of participation at every stage of the administrative process . . . as it did upon the measurement of the resulting IEP against a substantive standard.*

IEP teams need to meet with parents and consider their views, requests, opinions, and information—all in language parents can understand. Use plain language! Leave acronyms and jargon behind!

Practice Hint: If you do use acronyms, provide a list with definitions.

For IEPs, it's a good idea to remind team members of the purpose of the IDEA (20 USC 1400(d)(1)(A)):

> *to ensure that all children with disabilities have available to them a free appropriate public education that emphasizes special education and related services designed to meet their unique needs and prepare them for further education, employment, and independent living.*

23

What is the purpose of a 504 team meeting?

As part of regular education, 504 plans are designed to provide eligible students with disabilities the same opportunity to access, participate, and learn as their nondisabled peers have. Such plans often include accommodations, services, therapies, and even placements—whatever it takes to provide that opportunity.

Over the years, the OCR[7] has opined that Section 504 also provides a FAPE. Note that this requirement is not in the law, but is derived from years of practice in the field.

Note also that while this little flipbook of law calls 504 meetings team meetings, a more accurate designation is that they are 504 **group** or **committee** meetings. Check your state's practice!

---

[7]Again, see list of acronyms in the Appendix.

A 504 FAPE differs from an IDEA FAPE!

Unlike the IDEA, which is a "benefit" or "progress" statute, Section 504 is an "opportunity" statute. See further discussion below.

504 team members need to ask: how much opportunity is required? Answer: the same amount as **average** nondisabled peers are given. Some people may argue for more and may wish to have a 504 plan to help a student meet their potential. However, 504 does NOT require that. Though not illegal, providing more than required "violates" the **Pyramid of Laws**, discussed below.

> **Practice Hint:** IEPs provide an educational benefit according to *Rowley* and/or "progress appropriate in light of the child's circumstances" according to *Endrew F.*
>
> 504 plans provide an equal opportunity—equal to that of **average** nondisabled peers.

10 similarities between IEP and 504 team meetings

In preparing for any meeting, team members need to understand what a FAPE is under that specific law; what the job of the team is—and what it isn't, and how meetings differ under these two laws. With that knowledge, the IEP and 504 teams will provide what is legally required—no more and no less.

See the **Pyramid of Laws** in Figure 3.

Figure 3 Miriam's Pyramid of Laws

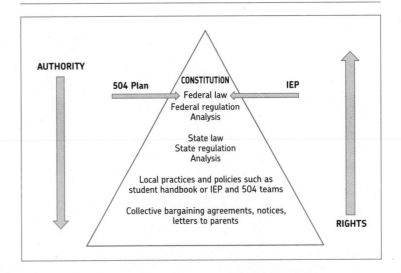

1. Miriam's Pyramid of Laws helps team members understand what the laws require and what goes beyond the requirements.

How does the Pyramid work? Teams should provide what is necessary and required—not more and not less. The Authority arrow (on the left side) shows that laws higher up on the Pyramid have more authority than those below. In contrast, the Rights arrow (on the right) goes from bottom to top and shows that rights can be added from bottom to top. Thus, *lower* laws, policies, and practices on the Pyramid CAN create more rights on IEPs and 504 plans than *higher* laws require!

> **Practice Hint:** Services that are included in IEPs or 504 plans, even if not legally mandated, rise to the level of federal law—and become like federal contracts. They need to be fully implemented by the school district. See that Pyramid again!

On the other hand, let's also remember that sometimes providing too much may not only be unnecessary but may also have unintended side effects for the student—the "Goldilocks Conundrum." These are discussed later.

2. Both laws are based on "group think."

IEPs and 504 plans are based on team decisions.[8] They are NOT developed by individuals—neither school personnel nor parents. Teams are groups of persons empowered to carry out two verbs:

1. **CONSIDER** what the child needs.
2. **DECIDE** what the school will provide to meet those needs.

[8]Note that a specific and limited IDEA exception allows schools and parents, by agreement, to make changes in an existing IEP without a meeting. See 20 USC 1414 (d)(1)(D); 34 CFR 300.324 (a)(4)(i).

What does "consider" mean?

Consider means that the team *discusses*, *reflects* upon, and *thinks* about, with a degree of care.

It does NOT mean that the team needs to adopt or follow what any team member may request. Nor does it mean that every team member must read every evaluation report or agree on all issues presented. A team meeting is NOT a democracy, where everyone gets a vote and everyone's opinions count the same. Indeed, no vote should be taken! A team meeting is the school's opportunity to offer services to provide the child with a FAPE. No more, no less.

Per *G.D. v. Westmoreland School District* (1st Cir. 1991) and *T.S. v. Board of Education of the Town of Ridgefield* (2nd Cir. 1993), considering an independent educational evaluation does not require a "substantive discussion."

In *R.Z.C. v. North Shore School District* (9th Cir. 2018, unpublished), the Court upheld the district's exiting a student with handwriting difficulties from special education, even though it contradicted the outside evaluator's conclusions.

Remember as well, per a long line of decisions, that a professional disagreement is not an IDEA violation—so long as the team *considered* input from its members. See again *F.L. v. Great Neck* (2018).

A veto is not the same as failure to consider or to predetermine a placement.

3. Both IEP and 504 Teams can end ("have closure") without consensus, that is, without having everyone in agreement.

This is because an IEP or a 504 plan is the school's proposal—not a compromise document. In both types of meetings, it's a document designed to provide a FAPE—under two different standards of FAPE: the IDEA's and 504's.

See, for example, *Murray v. Montrose County School District* (10th Cir. 1995), where the Circuit Court approved the IEP team meeting's process. At the time, team members could not reach agreement, so the school representative made the placement decision at the meeting, which then ended. Was that okay to do? The Circuit Court said, yes:

> *Because the staffing team could not reach consensus on the appropriate placement for Tyler, the ultimate decision fell to Mr. Binder as the director of special education* [he was the public agency representative].

Letter to Richards (OSEP 2010) had the same result.

Practice Hint: Don't take a vote at a team meeting!

---

4. IEP and 504 team meetings are designed to provide what a student NEEDS, not what a parent WANTS.

In *Park v. Anaheim Union High School District* (9th Cir. 2006), the Court found related services "beneficial," but not "necessary." They were NOT ordered.

In *M.G. v. Williamson County Schools* (6th Cir. 2018, unpublished), a parent provided the school with a doctor's prescription for occupational and physical therapy. However, the Court found that schools are not required to provide services for students who might benefit from those services. Rather, "the IDEA only requires schools to provide those services to students who **require** them in order to receive the full benefit of special education" [emphasis added].

5. Both meetings lead to a FAPE that belongs to the child, not the parents.

Letter to McKethan (OCR 1996) involves a common situation: a child is found eligible for an IEP but the parent wants the services on a 504 plan instead. The OCR found that once an IEP is developed for a student, the parent cannot compel the district to provide services on a 504 plan instead (34 CFR 104.33). A rejection of IEP services is also a rejection of 504 services, since one way for districts to comply with 504 is to comply with the IDEA. See also *Lamkin v. Lone Jack C-6 School District* (W.D. Mo. 2012), where parents couldn't bypass IDEA procedures by rejecting IDEA services and then requesting accommodations under 504.

In plain English: it's the team's job to determine what the student needs, not what the parents want (when that differs from the team's determination). The parents' recourse is to reject the IEP and proceed from there—not to compel the district to change its IEP.

> **Practice Hint:** Remember that the IEP or 504 plan is the district's plan for the child to receive a FAPE—not a compromise document. If parents dispute it, their recourse is to reject it and/or seek due process.

6. At both types of meetings, educators are the experts when it comes to teaching and learning.

Endrew F. underscores the reality that schools provide **expertise** while parents provide **input** in the development of the IEP.

To treat educators as experts, it's helpful to focus first on the WHAT and then on the WHO. The WHAT is the general curriculum, the standards, the requirements—that is, the material students are to learn. The WHO is the child and their needs.

The WHAT	The WHO
Each sport, game, or class has its own rules, goals, etc. To play and learn, you need to know them—the WHAT.	Each child is unique and has specific needs. The WHO is the child and their needs, etc.

The 1997 IDEA reauthorization introduced (and the 2004 IDEA continued) the congressional preference that most students with IEPs are to be educated in the "general curriculum." Thus, it's first the WHAT, and then the WHO.

1. Schools need to look at WHAT they teach in the general curriculum.
2. They then need to look at how to include the student (the WHO) appropriately.

This has always been so under Section 504, which is a regular education service.

Remember: educators are **experts** about the what and the who. Parents provide **input** about the who, not the what.

Keep the roles straight!

Courts defer to educators who testify with expertise about their knowledge and experience with the student.

In *T.B. v. Warwick* (2004), parents lost a methodology challenge in a case about a seven-year-old child with autism. The Court relied on the expertise of school personnel, as it found that the district had "well-trained teaching staff and a track record of success."

> **Practice Hint:** Document! Document! Data! Data! Data! How else did the Circuit Court know there was a record of success?

In *Watson v. Kingston City School District* (2nd Cir. 2005), the Circuit Court upheld the district's IEP, which used a "comprehensive multi-sensory approach" for a student with a learning disability and rejected the parents' evaluators' recommendation for a private school, using Orton-Gillingham:

> *The mere fact that a separately hired expert has recommended different programming does nothing to change this, as deference is paid to the District, not a third party.*

See also discussion earlier of *M.G. v. Williamson* (2018), where the Court found that the educators' numerous assessments were a better indicator of need than the child's doctor's prescription.

Alvin Independent School District (2007) includes an interesting discussion of teachers' firsthand knowledge of the child, in contrast to the physicians, who based their opinions on secondhand knowledge.

Endrew F. reminds us that courts "may fairly expect those [school] authorities to be able to offer a **cogent** and **responsive** explanation for their decisions that shows the IEP is reasonably calculated to enable the child to make progress in light of his circumstances."

With authority comes responsibility. You knew it did!

> **Practice Hint:** This responsibility to provide a "cogent and responsive" explanation requires staff training. Data! Data! Evidence-based methods, etc.

7. Inclusion—team members need to know what it involves.

1. They need to know the standards in the program—that is, the WHAT.

2. They need to know how to include the child appropriately—that is, how to educate the WHO.

More on the WHAT and the WHO

To do this, they need to know the difference between accommodations and modifications. These are changes in the general curriculum that provide access to students with disabilities so they can, like their nondisabled peers, participate and demonstrate what they know and can do.

To get started, let's define terms, starting with the umbrella term for all individualized changes in a student's IEP or 504 plan. This umbrella term is called an "adaptation" or "alteration."

Figure 4 Adaptation/Alteration

The **changes** may include a(n) accommodation, appropriate accommodation, nonstandard accommodation, modification, aids, benefits, and/or services. The terms "adaptation" or "alteration" do not involve the effect of each change on the validity of standards, requirements, tests, grades, etc.

Source: pixabay.com/kmicican

Fundamental alteration

This is a change that is so significant that it alters the essential nature of the course, subject, student requirement, standard, sport, or all other similar terms in school.

Examples: Using a calculator on an addition test, or reading a story to a student who is learning phonics and word decoding skills.

Validity

This is the requirement that the score or grade actually measures what it purports to measure.

For example, an "A" in science means that the student did the actual work of the class at a high level; the measure of the student's work was not fundamentally altered.

In testing, a test must be valid for the purpose with which it is used. Tests administered to students with disabilities "must be selected and administered so that the test accurately reflects what a student knows or is able to do, rather than a student's disability, except when the test is designed to measure disability-related skills," according to *North Carolina (NC) Department of Public Instruction* (OCR 2005), citing 504 and ADAAA requirements. Here, because the state writing test of convention is a valid means for testing writing skills, the use of dictation is not allowed.

Figure 5 Accommodation

Also known as the **standard** or
reasonable accommodation,
an accommodation is a change in course/test
presentation, location, timing, student
response, or other attribute that is
necessary to provide **access** for a student with
a disability to participate and demonstrate
their "academic achievement and functional
performance" and **does not fundamentally
alter** or lower the standard or expectations.

Accommodations preserve validity.

Figure 6 Modification

Also known as **nonstandard
accommodation**, a modification is a change
in course/test presentation, location, timing,
student response, or other attribute that is
necessary to provide **access** for a student with
a disability to participate and demonstrate
their "academic achievement
and functional performance" but that
fundamentally alters and/or lowers the
standard or expectations.

Modifications do NOT preserve validity.

See *Grading, Reporting, Graduating . . . and the Law* for a more detailed discussion of these important issues. Please visit **http://www.schoollawpro.com**.

A word about today's "good teaching" practices— creating some uncertainty for IEP and 504 teams

To determine eligibility or services, team members need to know what general education provides for ALL students. Many classrooms these days include "good teaching" approaches, such as universal design, evidence-based instruction, response to intervention (RTI), multi-tier systems of support (MTSS),[9] differentiated instruction, and other targeted approaches.

In most situations, there's no need to include these approaches in IEPs or 504 plans as they are available for ALL students and are not "specialized instruction" or adaptations/alterations. However (*and you knew this was coming!*), to ensure that those practices will, in fact, be used to meet the needs of a specific child, it's probably a good idea to include them.

> **Practice Hint:** Except when specifically needed by a student, as a general rule, don't include "good teaching" practices on IEPs or 504 plans. However, when in doubt—do!

---

[9]ESSA: "multi-tier system of support" means "a comprehensive continuum of evidence-based, systemic practices to support a rapid response to students' needs, with regular observation to facilitate data-based instructional decision-making" (20 USC 7801 (33)).

Read on for more clarity and direction from the OCR and OSEP.

Shelby County (TN) School District (OCR 2005) stated that there was no need for an IEP or a Section 504 plan, as the district provided classroom accommodations for all students.

In *Community Independent School District* (SEA Tex. 2004), regular education adaptations were appropriate. The student did not need special education or Section 504 services.

However, there was a difference with *Palm Beach County School Board* (SEA Fla. 2017). There, as the intensity of the student's needed interventions and resources far exceeded those available in the general education setting, an evaluation was likely in order.

Practice Hint: The better regular education, the fewer IEPs and 504 plans are needed.

8. Three practices Teams should avoid when providing a FAPE.

First, beware the Goldilocks Conundrum. This is when teams provide more than the child needs and ignore the *side effects* of doing so.

Usually, these extras are provided by people who mean well.

> Let's add this. It can't hurt.

Well, it can and often does.

44

Examples of the Goldilocks Conundrum

- Providing too many adaptations/alterations and compensatory strategies—instead of teaching the student specific skills.

- Overusing 1:1 aides. The student may learn to be helpless ("learned helplessness")

- Providing inflated grades (perhaps based on effort for this student, not achievement as for others in the class). These are actually a form of discrimination as they are based on the child's disability—not class standards or expectations.

See the following cases.

In *City of Chicago School District* (SEA Ill. 2013), they provided a calculator to the student instead of teaching him basic math skills. He received all passing grades, but the hearing officer was not impressed, as he concluded that the student could learn basic math skills with appropriate instruction. The hearing officer reminded the district that accommodations should help the student **learn** math skills and not replace specialized instruction.

On the other hand, see *Sherman and Nishanian v. Mamaroneck Union Free School District* (2nd Cir. 2003), where the district's refusal to provide a calculator was upheld because the calculator that the parents sought included all the functions the student was expected to learn. The school provided a

less sophisticated model so that educators could determine what the student had actually learned. The Court approved.

In *Montgomery Township Board of Education* (3rd Cir. 2005), passing grades were found to be based on overuse of accommodations and modifications, not the student's mastery of skills and knowledge.

In *Axelrod v. Phillips Academy* (D. Mass. 1999), the use of extended time was shown to be contraindicated as it did not help the student organize his time. The court analogized it to giving a later appointment to someone who is always late. Instead, the student should learn how to be on time!

In *A.C. v. Board of Education of the Chappaqua Central School District* (2nd Cir. 2009), regarding the use of a 1:1 aide, the Court undertook discussion of the overuse of accommodations and services that might lead to learned helplessness, reminding us that IEPs should aim for students' independence, not dependence on aids and benefits.

Second, avoid "compromise" IEPs and 504 plans that try to make parents happy but do not provide a FAPE to the student. Schools should avoid this practice because it may not provide a FAPE. They need to stay focused on their purpose!

Sometimes, as the saying goes, *"No good deed goes unpunished."*

...Continued

Third, team members need to remember whose meeting it is!

> **Question:** Is it the student's? The parent's? The district's?
>
> **Answer:** It's the district's meeting. The district is responsible for providing an IEP or a 504 plan, and the meeting is how it gets that job done.
>
> Who runs the meeting? **The district.**
>
> Who sets the agenda? **The district.**
>
> Who schedules it? **The district.**

Of course, the meeting proceeds at all stages (including scheduling) with input from parents, with due consideration of their input. That's why it's called a **team** meeting!

Some specifics

- Can parents request a meeting? **YES,** of course.
- Can parents demand a meeting? **NO,** not under the IDEA or Section 504. Under federal law, if the school does not believe a meeting is necessary, it does not need to schedule one. Check your state law on this.

  - Specifically, **under the IDEA**, the district needs to inform parents through prior written notice (PWN) why no meeting will be held. The parents can dispute that decision, as they can any decision that the district makes.

  - **Under Section 504**, the district needs to meet if the school has reason to believe the child may be eligible for 504 protection.

- Can parents demand that a meeting be scheduled at a specific time? **NO**. Under the IDEA, the meeting needs to be jointly scheduled. Section 504 is silent on how to schedule meetings. Districts should develop and follow local policies and practices.

- Can parents demand that a meeting end when they leave it? **Not usually**. In *Pangerl v. Peoria Unified School District* (9th Cir. 2019), parents had fully participated for two hours before they left. Continuing the meeting for twenty minutes did not "seriously infringe parent's opportunity to participate in the IEP formulation process."

Of course, you may want to offer a follow-up meeting. A good preventive practice!

See later discussion for the description of the IDEA's PWN.

9. Both types of meetings call for the use of plain language.

Teams should work to ensure that parents understand the team process, the student's current academic achievement and functional performance, the services that are proposed, their options, and so on. For evaluations under both laws and for the IEP process, educators need to know the four attributes of parental **consent** or **waiver** for any process, evaluations, services, or placement, in which districts request parental approval. (Note that parental consent is NOT required in order to implement a 504 plan.)

The consent or waiver must be:

1. Voluntary
2. Informed
3. Written
4. Revocable

See IDEA regulation, 34 CFR 300.9, and discussion of consent below.

In *Somoza v. New York City Department of Education* (D.S. N.Y. 2007) the *pro se*[10] parent signed a waiver of rights as part of a settlement agreement, but the District Court found that she did so not knowingly and not voluntarily, making the waiver ineffective.

---

[10]Please see Appendix for definition.

49

10. At both types of meetings, teams should:

- Leave acronyms outside the meeting, or explicitly define each.
- Speak clearly and simply in plain language.
- Provide a glossary for new terms; describe them explicitly.
- Offer to reconvene, if appropriate.
- Follow up with the parents, as appropriate.

Examples of plain language

Too complex—don't use!	Just right—use!
Oliver will participate in assessments.	Oliver will take tests.
Alice has learned word attack skills.	Alice has learned to read words.
The school affords Oliver the opportunity to . . .	The school allows Oliver (or provides Oliver) . . .
Alice will acquire knowledge.	Alice will learn.
I would appreciate if you would . . .	Please!

You get the idea! Keep it clear and simple!

Differences between IEP and 504 meetings

IDEA—a very prescriptive law. The law mandates who has to attend, when the team needs to meet, how it should proceed, etc.

Section 504—a much looser law. Every school district develops its own policies and practices.

First, let's discuss IEP meetings; then, 504 meetings.

IEP team meetings: Who, when, where, why, how

Who should attend?

Figure 7 Team Meeting Composition

- Parents of the child
- No fewer than one regular education teacher
- No fewer than one special education teacher
- LEA representative who is (1) qualified to provide/supervise provision of special education and (2) knowledgeable about general curriculum and LEA resources
- Individual who can interpret instructional implications of evaluation results
- Others with knowledge or special expertise
- Whenever appropriate, the child

Some additional requirements

The IDEA adds specific persons for meetings dealing with transitioning children from early childhood programs and for high schoolers transitioning to the next stage of their lives (34 CFR 300.321 (b) (1) and (f)). For the latter, the district must invite the "child with a disability if the purpose of the meeting will be" to consider postsecondary goals and transition services.

Be sure that team members understand the role of the school district's representative (who may or may not be the team chairperson).

4) *A representative of the public agency who—*

　(i) *Is qualified to provide, or supervise the provision of, specially designed instruction to meet the unique needs of children with disabilities;*

　(ii) *Is knowledgeable about the general education curriculum; and*

　(iii) *Is knowledgeable about the availability of resources of the public agency.*

(Authority: 20 USC 1414(d)(1)(B)–(d)(1)(D); 34 CAR 300.321)

In sum, the LEA representative can provide or supervise special education, knows the general curriculum, and is knowledgeable about the availability of resources.

Parental attendance—What the LEA needs to do to

Districts are to "take steps to assure that one or both parents of a child with a disability are present at each IEP team meeting or are afforded the opportunity to participate." Districts need to take specific steps and efforts to convince the parents to attend and to document their efforts (34 CFR 300.322).

In *Mr. and Mrs. M. v. Ridgefield Board of Education* (D. Ct. 2007), the district did not make necessary efforts to get the parents to attend, which the Court found to be a denial of a FAPE.

See also *In re Student with a Disability* (SEA Minn. 2018), where one letter and one voicemail sent two days before a scheduled IEP meeting were not enough notice for a mother to have the opportunity to attend and participate in her child's IEP meeting.

On the other hand, if a district takes appropriate steps to ensure parental participation and parents still don't attend, the district can proceed without them to develop the IEP. This long-established practice is consistent with the fact that it is the district's responsibility to provide a FAPE. The student has the right to have the meeting and to receive a FAPE. See, for example, *E.M. v. Pajaro Valley Unified School District* (N.D. Calif. 2007).

...Continued

Lathrop R-II School District v. Gray (8th Cir. 2010), citing 34 CFR 300.345: "If the public agency is unable to convince the parents to attend" the team meeting can proceed.

And finally, see the earlier discussion about if parents demand that the meeting end when they leave it, decided by *Pangerl v. Peoria* (2019). No violation was found because the parents had fully participated for two hours before they left. Continuing the meeting for twenty minutes did not "seriously infringe parents' opportunity to participate in the IEP formulation process."

What if some school folks don't attend?

It depends. It could be a significant issue. Many courts focus attention on the requirement that the **general education teacher** attend, finding that if the teacher is not present for the discussion of the program, the parents are denied the opportunity to participate in the development of the IEP, which may violate their FAPE rights. Remember that providing parents with an opportunity to participate meaningfully in the development of the IEP is the SECOND PRONG OF THE FAPE REQUIREMENT. Very important!

In *Westerville City Schools* (SEA Ohio 2016), the district violated the procedures for the team meeting by not appropriately excusing the general education teacher from the meeting and not obtaining input from the teacher in advance of the meeting.

See also *Anoka-Hennepin Independent School District #011* (SEA Minn. 2014) for the need to document IEP meeting attendees to be able to later prove that the meeting was properly constituted (34 CFR 300.321).

IEP team members need to understand the role of the regular educator(s) at the meeting.

To the extent appropriate (34 CFR 300.320 (a)(4)), participate in the development of the IEP for the child, including determining the following:

- Appropriate positive behavioral interventions and supports
- Other strategies for the child
- Supplementary aids and services
- Program modifications
- Support for school personnel

58

Specific exceptions—excusals and waivers

The IDEA allows teams to get their work done in some situations when some members do not attend. Use caution with these provisions (34 CFR 300.321 (e)(2)).

Figure 8 Excusing Attendance at Team Meeting

- Attendance not necessary.
- Attendance necessary, but excused.

Both require written agreement with parents. For **necessary but excused**, excused team members must submit written input to parents and other team members *before the meeting*.

To summarize

For **attendance not necessary**, the parents and school must *agree* that the person is not necessary. For **attendance necessary but excused**, the parents must *consent*—a higher threshold. Both the agreement in the first and the consent in the second need to be in writing.

Remember the adage "*If it's not in writing, it didn't happen.*"

Figure 9 Amending IEP Without Team Meeting

If . . .

- parent(s) and LEA agree not to convene AND

- team has already held annual meeting,

then . . .

- team may draft and execute IEP amendment but must incorporate into IEP at parent's request.

Remember that this is a specific exception to the general rule about these meetings (20 USC 1414 (d)(1)(D); 34 CFR 300.324 (a)(4)(i)).

The IEP team needs to understand what parental consent is and why it matters.

For IEPs, under the IDEA, parental consent is required before a child's initial placement (300 CFR 300.300 (a) through (c)). States may require more.

What is "consent"? Here's the IDEA definition (34 CFR 300.9, emphasis added):

Consent means that—

*(a)   The parent has been **fully informed of all information relevant** to the activity for which consent is sought, in his or her native **language,** or other mode of communication;*

*(b)   The parent **understands** and **agrees in writing** to the carrying out of the activity for which his or her consent is sought, and the consent describes that activity and lists the records (if any) that will be released and to whom; and*

*(c)(1)   The parent understands that the granting of consent is **voluntary** on the part of the parent and **may be revoked** at anytime.*

*(2)   If the parent revokes consent, that **revocation is not retroactive** (i.e., it does not negate an action that has occurred after the consent was given and before the consent was revoked).*

*(3)   If the parent **revokes consent in writing** for their child's receipt of special education services after the child is initially provided special education and related services, the public agency is **not required** to amend the child's education records to remove any references to the child's receipt of special education and related services because of the revocation of consent.*

...Continued

It's helpful to think of consent as "informed consent," and it's the district's job to inform parents of their rights to consent or to waive services.

The 2006 IDEA regulations allow parents to revoke consent in writing for special education and related services at any time (34 CFR 300.9 (c)(3)). Schools may not continue to provide services after the parents revoke consent and may not, under federal law, seek due process to compel services.

Also, if parents refuse to consent to an initial evaluation or an initial placement, the district is not required to provide a FAPE to the child. Check state law about what the district should do in these situations.

Schools need to provide parents with prior written notice (PWN) before ceasing the services (34 CFR 300.503). See later discussion.

After parents refuse to consent for special education, federal law makes clear that henceforth, the child will be considered a general education student and that LEAs will not be considered to be violating their responsibility to make a FAPE available.

This is an important IDEA issue (but not under 504, as before implementing 504 plans, schools do not need parental consent unless local or state law requires it).

Back to basics about consent

Here is a decision about the possible effects of a parent's refusal to consent for an evaluation.

In *Fairfield Board of Education* (SEA Conn. 2016), the parent refused to provide consent for an evaluation, which led to a denial of a FAPE—in this case, caused by the parent. Thus, when the parent sought reimbursement for a private placement, that refusal was deemed "unreasonable," given the equities involved. Reimbursement was not granted.

As attorney Jim Walsh says, *"Being reasonable is always a good idea!"*

Use care when dealing with consent and waiver issues!

Finally, the IDEA's PWN requirement means that parents are entitled to know what the LEA is doing or not, and why.

The LEA needs to provide the parents with notice whenever it proposes to initiate a change or refuses to make a change about the identification, evaluation, educational placement, or FAPE for the child that includes

- a description of the action proposed or refused;

- an explanation of why the school is doing what it is doing;

- a description of other options considered and reasons they were rejected;

- a description of each evaluation procedure, test, record, or report the district used for its decision; other factors relevant to the district's decision;

- a statement of the parents' protection under the procedural safeguards of the law;

- if not an initial evaluation or referral, the way parents can obtain the procedural safeguards; and

- sources where parents can get help in understanding the law and their rights.

Practice Hint: Wrightslaw, a parent advocacy/information website, has the following anagram about smart IEPs—useful for parents and schools.

Goals on IEP need to be SMART:

S-Specific

M-Measurable

A-Action words

R-Realistic

T-Time specific

Source: From Emotion to Advocacy, 2nd Ed., www.wrightslaw.com

Two more SMART realities.

> **First,** teams should have a good baseline from which to build goals for the student. Again, it's important to know what's going on in general education and where the child fits into that.

65

Second, school personnel should not stray beyond their area of expertise in describing the child, recommendations, concerns, and so forth. For example, a speech therapist who attempts to "diagnose" depression or recommend psychotherapy diminishes their credibility. **Just don't do it!**

The IEP team needs to consider the essential components of reading instruction that Congress added to foster explicit and systemic instruction.

See definition in Section 1208(3) of the *Elementary and Secondary Education Act* (ESEA):

(A) phonemic awareness

(B) phonics

(C) vocabulary development

(D) reading fluency, including oral reading skills

(E) reading comprehension strategies

Check state law regarding dyslexia. This is an active area of rapid change these days. See also *Letter to Unnerstall* (OSEP 2016) and *Dear Colleague Letter* (ED 2015, October 23).

The IEP team needs to consider "evidence-based interventions" as defined in the ESSA (from section 8101 (21)(A) of the ESEA).

"[T]he term 'evidence-based,' when used with respect to a State, local educational agency, or school activity, means an activity, strategy, or intervention that—

(i) *demonstrates a statistically significant effect on improving student outcomes or other relevant outcomes based on—*

    (I) *strong evidence from at least one well-designed and well-implemented experimental study;*

    (II) *moderate evidence from at least one well-designed and well-implemented quasiexperimental study; or*

    (III) *promising evidence from at least one well-designed and well-implemented correlational study with statistical controls for selection bias; or*

...Continued

      (ii) (I) *demonstrates a rationale based on high-quality research findings or positive evaluation that such activity, strategy, or intervention is likely to improve student outcomes or other relevant outcomes; and*

      (II) *includes ongoing efforts to examine the effects of such activity, strategy, or intervention."*

For further guidance, see **https://www2.ed.gov/policy/elsec/leg/essa/guidanceuseseinvestment .pdf**; **https://www.edglossary.org/evidence-based/**; **https://www.cde.ca.gov/re/es/evidence.asp**.

How do we do this at team meetings?

Basically: Let's remember that especially since *Endrew F.,* school personnel need to provide a "cogent and responsive explanation for their decisions." What does that mean?

Team members need to be able to answer these questions (essentially the same question):

- *Why are you using this method, approach, product, or system to teach my child?*

- *What evidence supports your approach?*

- *How will your method help my child progress appropriately in light of my child's circumstances? Tell me in plain language!*

In short, the IEP team needs evidence that the program it proposes is reasonably calculated to help the child progress appropriately. Schools should be able to provide evidence of peer-reviewed research to the extent practicable, particularly when proposing programs for teaching reading—as much research exists about that skill area (20 USC 1414 (d)(1)(A)(i)(IV)).

ESSA uses the term "evidence-based interventions."

Later, we discuss how these terms are used and defined. It's an ever-changing area of law and practice.

For a cautionary tale, see *Tuscaloosa County Board of Education* (SEA Ala. 2017), where school personnel were unable to provide a "cogent and responsive explanation" for their program.

Once in the IEP, be sure to implement the program with fidelity—according to its specifications.

Figure 10 "With Fidelity"

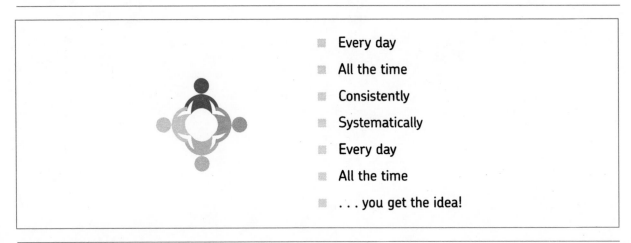

- Every day
- All the time
- Consistently
- Systematically
- Every day
- All the time
- . . . you get the idea!

Source: pixabay.com/Clker-Free-Vector-Images

Eight day-to-day practicalities for the IEP process

Of course, the overriding requirement is that the team carry out two verbs—to CONSIDER and to DECIDE. The team needs to CONSIDER all relevant information and to DECIDE what the child's IEP will include (and, if asked, provide a "cogent and responsive explanation" for its decision).

Alas, over the years, we've seen that these two verbs are easier said than done!

Here's more . . .

First: The key requirement for the IEP team is that parents have the opportunity to participate meaningfully in the development of the IEP.

Schools need to provide parents with the opportunity to participate in the development of the IEP. They need to be able to provide input and share their views, information, and requests, and the team needs to consider these. *Endrew F.* reminds us that parents **provide input** while school personnel **provide expertise**.

LEAs need to do what it takes to ensure the above—including speaking in plain language (perhaps hiring a translator), defining terms and acronyms, hiring a "mentor," etc.

...Continued

On the other hand, it does not mean that the team should take a vote or adopt the parents' opinion or preference. Recall that the operating verb is **consider**. And recall that a professional disagreement does not mean that the parents' input was not considered.

See *G.D. v. West Chester Area School District* (E.D. Pa. 2017), where an intellectually gifted third grader with an anxiety disorder was found ineligible for special education, in spite of the parents' evaluator's recommendation and the parents' dispute with the school's psychologist.

And see again *F.L. v. Great Neck*, stating—as have a long line of court decisions—that a professional disagreement is not an IDEA violation.

It's a two-way street. Parents need to be open about what they want and need to participate in the development of the IEP.

In *Ellenberg v. New Mexico Military Institute* (10th Cir. 2007), the parents never asked the team for an IEP or requested that an earlier IEP be revised. Instead, they placed their child in a private school and sought reimbursement. The Court dismissed their claim, as they had NOT exhausted the IEP process.

See also *M.S. v. Mullica Township Board of Education* (3rd Cir. 2018), where the parent's refusal to cooperate with the team process barred her reimbursement claim.

Similar results were found in *C.G. and B.S. v. Five Town Community School District* (1st Cir. 2008). The IEP was still being developed when the parents filed their due process complaint seeking payment for their unilateral placement. The Court denied their reimbursement claim for failing to cooperate with the team process.

See also *Doe v. Cape Elizabeth School Department* (D.C. Me. 2019), where the school's failure to meet the initial evaluation deadline was excused by the parents' failure to make the student available.

Reasonableness cuts both ways!

But see *R.S. v. Board of Directors of Woods Charter School Company* (M. D. N. C. 2019). The Court held that the fact that parents were difficult to deal with did not relieve the school from the responsibility to develop an IEP.

Second: Be sure to provide prior written notice (PWN) (34 CFR 300.503).

There's been much litigation and guidance on this requirement. For example, *Letter to Chandler* (OSEP 2012) reminds the district that the prior written notice needs to be timely.

And see *Mesa County Valley School District* (2016), where a district failed to provide the PWN to parents of a student with autism when it changed his placement to a therapeutic day program.

Third: School personnel can have a pre-team huddle before the team meeting.

In fact, such a meeting is often a good idea, so long as no DECISION is made there! Pre-team meetings can review data, progress reports, evaluations, options, opinions, etc. Notably, the regulations specifically exclude "preparatory activities that public agency personnel engage in to develop a proposal or response to a parent proposal that will be discussed at a later meeting" from the definition of a "meeting" (34 CFR 300.501 (b)(3)).

...Continued

Lee's Summit R-VII School District (SEA Mo. 2012) provides a good example of a pre-team meeting.

See also *Mamaroneck Union Free School District* (2nd Cir. 2009). Team members need to come with an open mind—but can discuss services before meeting.

In *T.W. v. Unified School District # 259* (10th Cir. 2005) the Circuit Court found that school officials should come to the table with an **open mind**, but this does not mean they should come with an **"empty" mind**.

Fourth: The district may come to the meeting with a draft IEP.

See *Fuhrmann v. East Hanover Board of Education* (3rd Cir. 1993). A draft IEP can be approved, so long as it's truly a draft with the expectation that it can be revised at the team meeting where the parents' input will be considered.

In sum, consider a pre-IEP team meeting if you need to do the following:

- Clarify issues for the team meeting

- Identify concerns that are known, both of school personnel and of the parents

- Develop a draft IEP

- Be sure school personnel know what a FAPE is and what the team process will be

- Be sure all members know that "consider" and "decide" are the operative verbs

- Be sure general education personnel can describe the curriculum and what are modifications or accommodations

- Prepare for behavioral challenges or potentially disruptive personal issues

Fifth: Predetermination is a resounding NO! Team members may NOT make decisions before the team meeting about what the school will offer.

Having team members come to the meeting with a decision already made is called "predetermination" and violates the purpose and spirit of these meetings. Courts guard the

process and often find predetermination to be a denial of a FAPE. Why? Because the team did not CONSIDER and DECIDE. See *R.L. v. Miami-Dade County Schools* (11th Cir. 2014).

But see *Hjortness v. Neenah Joint School District* (7th Cir. 2007), where the Circuit Court rejected the parents' argument that the district predetermined the child's placement by not considering the private placement after the team found the less restrictive public school placement appropriate. The Court found that the parents' rights to participate in the development of the IEP were not infringed in any meaningful way.

Deal v. Hamilton County Board of Education (6th Cir. 2004) is a case about program predetermination for a student with autism. The parents sought applied behavioral analysis (ABA) instead of the district's eclectic program. The Court determined that the district, having predetermined the placement, did not consider the parents' request. The decision dealt with procedural issues and was remanded to determine the substantive placement. *Deal v. Hamilton County Board of Education* (2008) affirmed the earlier decision.

...Continued

Sixth: Remember that a professional disagreement is not an IDEA violation—as discussed earlier.

> **Practice Hint**: Of course, it may be a great idea for staff members to be proactive when they sense that parents are not happy with the child's services or proposed program—perhaps when the parents hire an evaluator or refuse to consent to school evaluations or services. Often a good idea in those cases is to meet with the parents or reconvene the team to consider the parents' concerns.

Seventh: The least restrictive environment (LRE)—what do courts say?

Congress's preference is for children with IEPs to be educated in the LRE to the maximum extent **appropriate** with children who are not disabled (20 USC 1412 (a)(5); 34 CFR 300.114).

LRE is a subject unto itself as standards continually shift. **Keep up with decisions in your state and circuit!** Courts often weigh the benefits of inclusion in the general curriculum, the learning/ progress that the child is reasonably expected to make, and the level of disruption the child may create in that classroom. Schools need to make efforts to include students in the school they would have attended if not for the IEP; collect data about that effort; make accommodations and modifications, if needed; and provide a program where the child can progress appropriately in light

of their circumstances. Some courts reason that schools do not need to set up parallel programs in regular classrooms that may be, as one court termed it, "beyond recognition." As a general rule, focus on FAPE benefit/progress! The following are sample decisions.

C.D. v. Natick (2019) highlighted again that the LRE is a congressional preference—not a mandate. A child's program needs to be appropriate. In this case, placement in a self-contained classroom for academics was deemed appropriate.

In *R.F. v. Cecil County Public Schools* (4th Cir. 2019), parents' request for the child to be only with other disabled peers contradicted the law's LRE preference. Thus, they lost their tuition reimbursement request.

In *L.H. v. Hamilton County Department of Education* (6th Cir. 2018), the Court rejected the district's notion that mainstreaming is appropriate only if the student can master the grade-level curriculum. "The appropriate yardstick is whether the child, with appropriate supplemental aids and services, can make progress toward the IEP's goals in the regular education setting."

In *Solorio v. Clovis Unified School District* (9th Cir. 2019, unpublished), the Court found that the LRE preference was met for a child with Down syndrome. The district placed the child in a segregated classroom for half the day for academics and in the general education classroom for the remainder of the day for socialization.

Thus, a district's change in the "location" of a program is not a change in "placement" triggering IDEA procedures such as the reconvening of the IEP team. See *Spring Branch District* (2018).

Eighth: A word about the "stay-put"—another key IDEA right.

It means that, if there's a dispute between the school and parents, the student has the right to remain in the last agreed-upon placement until the dispute is resolved.

A recent decision, *L.J. v. School Board of Broward County Florida* (11th Cir. 2019), held that stay-put is satisfied when a district provides the significant elements of the child's program, even if not every element is provided. This Eleventh Circuit decision is also reflected in decisions in the Fourth, Fifth, Eighth, and Ninth Circuits.

This also is a very hot area of litigation that goes beyond the scope of this little flipbook of law.

Section 504 team meetings

The meeting is made up of a "group of persons knowledgeable about" three factors: the student, evaluation data, and the available resources.

Interestingly, federal law does not specifically mention the parents as 504 group members (34 CFR 104.35 (c)(3)). Check with your state law on this. **Miriam's Pyramid of Laws** in Figure 3 shows that states can provide *more* than the federal law, not *less*. Of course, in the real world of relationship building, it is generally good practice to include parents!

504 plans are designed to provide equal access for "otherwise qualified" individuals with a disability. Note that "plan," "group," "committee," and "team" all appear without capitalization. The words "team," "committee," and "group" are used interchangeably here. The 504 law does not require *written* plans. Again, in the real world, if the district develops a 504 plan, it's a good idea to have it in writing in order to prove its existence later, if needed.

Remember: *"If it's not in writing, it didn't happen."*

Figure 11 Section 504 of the *Rehabilitation Act of 1973*, 29 U.S.C § 794 (A)

> "No otherwise qualified individual with a disability . . . shall solely by the reason of her or his disability, be excluded from the participation in, be denied the benefits of, or be subjected to discrimination under any program or activity receiving federal financial assistance."

...Continued

An otherwise qualified individual is able to meet the **essential** requirements of the course, school—whatever. The law provides equal access, not advantage.

In *A.H. v. Illinois High School Association* (7th Cir. 2018), the state association was not required to lower standards for participation in the state track championships or to create a separate category for para-ambulatory athletes. That would fundamentally alter the event (therefore, it would be a modification) and 504 does not require modifications. It does require *accommodations*, as appropriate.

In *P.F. v. Stanford Taylor* (7th Cir. 2018), Wisconsin's Open Enrollment policy was found to not discriminate on the basis of disability even though it accepted students with or without IEPs on a *different* basis. The policy required that the receiving district have "excess capacity" to serve incoming students. Thus, the basis for those with IEPs was the existence of appropriate programming for them. To demand that districts create programs that don't exist would require a "fundamental alteration" of the program. Again, not a 504 requirement.

Here too, the WHAT rules! It's all about the WHAT first. Then the WHO.

WHO is a "disabled person"?

Section 504 of the ADAAA, 42 USC 12101 *et seq*.

A "***disabled person***". . . *has a physical or mental **impairment** which **substantially limits** one or more **major life activities** of such individual; has a record of such impairment; or being regarded as having such an impairment.* [emphasis added]

---

504 plans are developed for students who have an **impairment** that **substantially limits** one or more **major life activities** AND who **need accommodations and/or services as a result**. The ADAAA expanded list of "major life activities" includes "operations of a major bodily function." Note that these lists are not exhaustive. As well, students whose impairments are episodic or in remission may now be eligible for 504 plans. See *Frequently Asked Questions About Section 504 and the Education of Children With Disabilities* (OCR 2015).

...Continued

Note again that 504 plans are developed for students who meet all criteria mentioned above, not those who are merely "regarded as having" or "have a record of" impairment.

When making 504 eligibility determinations, use the baseball analogy, "running the bases." To be eligible for a 504 plan, a student needs to run the bases and get "home."

The analogy works because just about everyone knows the difference between getting to first, second, or third base and getting home. **So, how does it work?**

To get to first base—need an **impairment**. Under the ADAAA, mitigation (except for glasses) may not be considered.

To get to second base—need a **major life activity** (such as learning, reading, thinking, concentrating, breathing,

Source: pixabay.com/Clker-Free-Vector-Images

walking, talking, seeing, working with one's hands, hearing, etc.). Life activities are global—not spelling, math, or test anxiety, for example (28 CFR 35.108 (a)(1)(i)).

To get to third base—need a **limitation** resulting from that impairment.

To get "home"—need the limitation to be **substantial**, when compared to "most people in the general population" (28 CFR 35.108 (d)(1)(v)).

Only a student who gets "home" is eligible for a 504 plan.

Note, however, that students with a disability (who get to third base) may be "technically eligible" for general antidiscrimination provisions, even though they do not need aids or services. See *Dear Colleague Letter* (OCR 2012).

Figure 12 What Is Substantial?

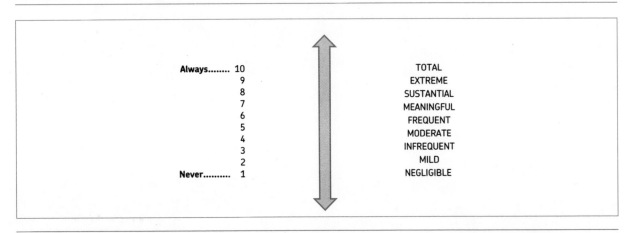

Source: Adapted from Dr. Perry Zirkel.

> **Practice Hint:** To make 504 eligibility determinations, separate the word "impairment" from "disability." The ADAAA makes this distinction more useful and important than ever.

- An **impairment** is a medical, psychological, psychiatric, or educational diagnosis.
- A **disability** is a legal conclusion made by the school-based 504 team. It's a judgment call, based on information about how the child is functioning.

An evaluator can provide expertise about the impairment. Parents can provide **input** about the child. Educators can provide **expertise** about what the school is teaching and the child.

Only the 504 group can determine whether the child needs a 504 plan.

Bear in mind five attributes of Section 504 plans.

First, they are not supposed to provide an unfair advantage.

In *PGA Tour Inc. v. Casey Martin* (2001), the Supreme Court allowed Casey Martin, the golfer, to use the golf cart as an accommodation. The Court reasoned, among other factors, that it did not give him an unfair advantage. If the cart had done so, the Court would not have allowed it.

Second, they generally include necessary services and adaptations that are not already provided by schools for all students.

But note that individual situations may require that those services and adaptations be included in a 504 plan.

Third, 504 plans do not need to be accepted by parents in order to be implemented.

504 plans provide accommodations and services in order for the district not to discriminate against a student with a disability. It's been long established that a district does not need parental consent to provide accommodations or services under federal law. Check your state's laws and practices, and keep abreast of OCR letters about a "change in placement"—as they may impact this practice.

On the other hand, while the law does not require it, the OCR has opined that schools need to get parental consent before the initial evaluation of a child under Section 504.

Fourth, 504 plans do not provide "stay-put" rights.

This is an important difference from the IDEA's IEPs.

Fifth, parents have the right to dispute the district's action.

Parents have due process rights to dispute 504 plans through procedures set up by the LEA, the state, and/or the OCR. The school district needs to inform parents about their rights.

In summary, here are some No's under Section 504

Figure 13 No's under 504

To figure out who is eligible as a "disabled person" under a 504 plan, do NOT:

- Conflate "impairment" with "disability"
- Use boilerplate accommodations
- Give too many accommodations
- Think there are "stay put" rights
- Include good teaching practices on 504 plans unless the student specifically needs them
- Write a 504 as a consolation prize when an IEP is not provided

To see a template version of a 504 plan, please visit the companion website to this book.

Good practices for both types of meetings

A. Prepare for meetings. *Preparation, preparation!*

- Invite the necessary participants.

- Prepare an agenda.

- Locate a comfortable room that is large enough for all. Is the table welcoming (with flowers) or is it a mess (crumpled up papers, stacks of papers, etc.)? Make it attractive and welcoming. How about some water for everyone?

- Seat participants appropriately and, when needed, strategically. (Do we really need to sit in tiny chairs?)

- Prepare team members before the meeting to understand their roles, the process, and what FAPE is (and isn't).

B. Know the "cringe words." Don't use them at team meetings.

- "We don't have that type of therapy here."

- "Because this is the method that I'm certified in."

- "I don't know if we can do that. I'll check and get back to you."

- "I don't have time in my schedule to provide that service."

- "I'm not a psychologist, but I think Tom is depressed."

- "He needs three hours of therapy, but we can't fit it into our schedule."

- "I don't discriminate. I treat everyone exactly the same in my classes."

- "We want what's best for your child." Avoid this! It overpromises and will, undoubtedly, underdeliver and kill trust. While it may sound nice, it's not what the law requires.

- Never say "never"! Instead, say, "We'll consider it."

C. Develop and follow an agenda and ground rules.

- Get team members' agreement on ground rules before the meeting starts.

- Start and end on time!

- Do not allow interruptions or side conversations.

- Respect others; maintain confidentiality.

- Turn phones and pagers off. If you're expecting an urgent call, inform team members BEFORE the phone rings!

- Track issues agreed upon—perhaps use a flipchart or computer program.

- Announce when the meeting is soon to end so members can wind down and discuss next steps.

D. Chair the meeting appropriately.

The team leader or chairperson

- represents the district, understands the process, and manages the group to keep the focus on developing the plan;
- provides the procedural safeguards to the parents;
- sets out the purpose of the meeting, the "big picture";
- sets behavioral expectations for all members before the meeting;
- assists school personnel to be professional and cordial;
- controls the meeting, takes caucuses or orderly breaks, if appropriate;
- paces the meeting and ends it on time;
- makes sure everyone understands next steps; and
- reschedules to complete the work, if needed.

In short, the chairperson's job is to focus everyone's attention on the future—the plan that is being developed, not the past.

...Continued

Think of Wayne Gretzky, the great hockey player. When asked why he was so successful, he is said to have answered, "I skate to where the puck is going to be, not where it's been."

Source: pixabay.com/mohamed_hassan

**Here too, focus on where the team is heading and
what the student needs going forward.**

E. And there's more! Mother was right! School personnel should follow her sage advice.

- Be on time. Don't keep parents and colleagues waiting.

- Start with friendliness. A smile always helps. Introduce everyone.

- Watch body language, especially rolling eyes, frowns, sighs, facial expressions, gum chewing, rudeness.

- Don't slouch.

- Make no promises you cannot keep.

- Follow up! Inform parents of their rights. Call or offer to meet with them to clarify confusion or concerns and to explain the process for mediation, hearings, and so on.

- Return phone calls.

In short, work to build and maintain **TRUST** with families. Work to build positive relationships. Be kind. Be reasonable. Be present. Know the legal requirements. **WHY?** Because this is a relationship business and **TRUST** is the coin of the realm. Without it, education becomes ever more challenging and fraught with tension; with it, schools and families work collaboratively to benefit the child. Let's go for that!

F. What does a good meeting look like?

- Agenda is followed.
- Chairperson exerts leadership.
- Members practice active listening—even when they dispute the opinion of others.
- Members acknowledge differences of opinion and the emotional nature of issues.
- Members understand the basics, such as what a FAPE is—and isn't.
- Members learn how to deliver bad news—about grades, behavior, etc.
- Schedule is maintained. Meeting ends on time.
- Members are encouraged to be succinct, defuse challenging situations, and focus on the plan.
- Paraphrase, clarify, "I hear you saying that . . . "
- Use the "parking lot." Leave that issue for another time. Move on.

G. What can go wrong at meetings

WHAT IF . . .	WHAT TO DO
Parents show up with an attorney—without notifying the school in advance.	Give them the option to proceed without the attorney or reschedule meeting so parents' and school's attorneys can attend. But check OSEP guidance that meeting not be postponed.
Parents bring a tape recorder without prior notice.	It depends on your state law, local policies, and procedures. If a tape recorder is necessary for parental access, it's allowed. The district should have its own as well.
Tempers flare.	Take a break. Do NOT tolerate intimidation or aggressive behavior! You may need to reschedule if members cannot act respectfully.
A team member tries to take over.	Refer everyone to the agreed-upon (hopefully, written) procedures. If member doesn't comply, interrupt and rephrase what speaker says.
A team leader expects disruption.	Discuss contingencies in advance with administrators or security personnel.
Educator speaks outside area of expertise.	Don't!
Participant cries, becomes emotional.	Acknowledge emotion. Take a break. If appropriate, end meeting and reconvene later.

And more things that can go wrong. . . .

WHEN . . .	WHAT TO DO
Conflict emerges.	Deal! That's the nature of the business. Don't ignore.
Parents and school disagree.	School representative decides. Remember, the meeting can close without consensus and a professional disagreement is not a denial of a FAPE!
The child's parents don't like each other and/or disagree with each other.	Stay neutral; don't take sides. Take a break if needed.
Conflicts emerge that are unresolved.	Say something like, "We need to move on. We need to agree to disagree."
When parents dispute a team decision.	Inform them of their rights, including mediation, resolution meeting, and hearings. Offer to meet them after meeting to clarify, assist, etc.
The agenda is not completed by the time the meeting is to end.	Reconvene; or, when appropriate, offer to meet with parents informally.

*Thank you to Nancy Kolb, *Things That "Go Bump" in the Meeting*. Professional Development, CASE/EDCO/LABBB, Waltham MA.

H. If you are really concerned about
how the team meeting will go . . .

Make it welcoming and friendly. Serve a snack! There's nothing like a nice glass of cold water or a cup of hot coffee to ease tensions and create a more productive atmosphere.

I. After the meeting—

- Follow up. Contact parents to see if they have concerns or questions. Taking this step has been known to defuse many a dispute and help to avoid due process. Why? It's a positive relationship builder.

- Reconvene if circumstances change. For example: if the child is not progressing as expected; if the child is making more progress than expected; if the child is not accessing accommodations or services; if the child is absent a lot, or sick, or if there is any other meaningful change.

- Take a deep breath and smile. You've done your best. You have an amazing opportunity to serve students and provide excellent education for all—and you are doing exactly that! Our nation thanks you!

Glossary

504   Section 504 of the *Rehabilitation Act of 1973*; also known as Section 504

ADAAA   *Americans with Disabilities Act Amendments Act*, 42 USC 12101–12210 (also known as ADAA)

CFR   Code of Federal Regulations (the regulations)

ED   United States Department of Education (also known as DoE)

ESEA   *Elementary and Secondary Education Act of 1965* (part of the Great Society legislation); has been reauthorized many times, including as part of the NCLB and ESSA

ESSA   *Every Student Succeeds Act*, enacted in 2015

FAPE   free appropriate public education

FCR   Federal Code of Regulations (the regulations)

IDEA   *Individuals with Disabilities Education Act*

IDELR   Individuals with Disabilities Education Law Report

...Continued

IEP	Individualized Education Program
LEA	local education agency; generally, the school district
NCLB	No Child Left Behind, enacted in 2001
OCR	Office for Civil Rights of the US ED
OSEP	Office for Special Education Programs of the US ED
OSERS	Office for Special Education Rehabilitative Services of the US ED
pro se	parent who is not represented by an attorney; "for him/herself"
PWN	prior written notice
USC	United States Code (the law)

Additional Resources

Eason, A., & Whitbread, K. (2006). *IEP and inclusion tips for parents and teachers.* IEP Resources.

Fisher, R., Ury, W., & Patton, B. (n.d.). Getting to YES. *Harvard Negotiation Project.* http://www.pon.harvard.edu.

Freedman, M. K. (2017). *Special education 2.0.—Breaking taboos to build a NEW education law.* School Law Pro.

Freedman, M. K. (2018). Waterstone's Endrew F.: Symbolism and reality from the schools' perspective. *Journal of Law and Education, 47*(4).

Freedman, M. K. (2020). *Grading, reporting, graduating and the law.* Corwin.

Giangreco, M. F., Edelman, S. W., Luiselli, T. E., & MacFarland, S. Z. C. (1997). Helping or hovering? Effects of instructional assistant proximity on students with disabilities. *Exceptional Children, 64*(1), 7–18.

Klor, G. (2007). *Say the right thing: A guide for responding to parents' IEP requests.* LRP Publications.

Kolb, N. (n.d.). *Things that "go bump" in the meeting.* Professional Development, CASE/EDCO/LABBB.

Sinek, S. (2009). *Start with WHY—How great leaders inspire everyone to take action.* Penguin.

Some good websites to visit: www.ed.gov; www.lrp.com; www.schoollawpro.com; www.wrightslaw.com.

References and Cases

A.C. v. Board of Education of the Chappaqua Central School District, 51 IDELR 147 (2nd Cir. 2009).

A.H. v. Illinois High School Association, 881 F.3d 587, 71 IDELR 121 (7th Cir. 2018).

Alvin Independent School District v. A.D., 48 IDELR 240 (5th Cir. 2007).

Anoka-Hennepin Independent School District #011, 114 LRP 37490 (SEA Minn. 2014).

Axelrod v. Phillips Academy, 30 IDELR 516 (D. Mass. 1999).

Board of Education of Hendrick Hudson Central School District v. Rowley, 458 U.S. 176, 553 IDELR 656 (1982).

Board of Education of Montgomery County v. S.G., 47 IDELR 285 (4th Cir. 2007).

C.D. v. Natick Public School District, 924 F.3d 621, 74 IDELR 121 (1st Cir. 2019).

C.G. and B.S. v. Five Town Community School District, 49 IDELR 93 (1st Cir. 2008).

City of Chicago School District, 62 IDELR 220 (SEA Ill. 2013).

Community Independent School District, 42 IDELR 244 (SEA Tex. 2004).

Deal v. Hamilton County Board of Education, 42 IDELR 109 (6th Cir. 2004); 49 IDELR 123 (6th Cir. 2008).

Dear Colleague Letter, 58 IDELR 79 (OCR 2012).

Dear Colleague Letter (OSEP 2015, October 23).

Dear Colleague Letter (OSEP 2015, November 16).

...Continued

D.L. v. Clear Creek Independent School District, 70 IDELR 32 (5th Cir. 2017).

Doe v. Board of Education of the Tullahoma City Schools, 20 IDELR 617 (6th Cir. 1993).

Doe v. Cape Elizabeth School Department, 74 IDELR 95 (D.C. Me. 2019).

Durbrow v. Cobb County School District, 72 IDELR 1 (11th Cir. 2018).

Edinburg (TX) Consolidated Independent School District, 49 IDELR 170 (OCR 2007).

Ellenberg v. New Mexico Military Institute, 47 IDELR 153, 478 F.3d 1262 (10th Cir. 2007).

E.M. v. Pajaro Valley Unified School District, 48 IDELR 39 (N.D. Calif. 2007).

Endrew F. v. Douglas County School District RE 1, 137 S. Ct. 988, 69 IDELR 174 (US 2017).

E.R. v. Spring Branch Independent School District, 909 F.3d 754, 73 IDELR 112 (5th Cir. 2018).

Fairfield Board of Education, 69 IDELR 21 (SEA Conn. 2016).

F.L. v. Board of Education of the Great Neck Union Free School District, 735 F. App'x 38, 72 IDELR 232 (2nd Cir. 2018).

Frequently Asked Questions about Section 504 and the Education of Children with Disabilities, 67 IDELR 189 (OCR 2015).

Fuhrmann v. East Hanover Board of Education, 993 F.2d 1031, 19 IDELR 1065 (1993).

G.D. v. West Chester Area School District, 70 IDELR 180 (E.D. Pa. 2017).

G.D. v. Westmoreland School District, 930 F.2d 942, 17 IDELR 751 (1st Cir. 1991).

Grim v. Rhinebeck Central School District, 346 F.3d 377 (2nd Cir. 2003).

...Continued

Hjortness v. Neenah Joint School District, 48 IDELR 119 (7th Cir. 2007).

Hood v. Encinitas Union School District, 486 F.3d 1099, 47 IDELR 213 (9th Cir. 2007).

In re Student with a Disability, 74 IDELR 184 (SEA Minn. 2018).

K.D. v. Downingtown Area School District, 904 F.3d 248, 72 IDELR 261 (3rd Cir. 2018).

Lamkin v. Lone Jack C-6 School District, 58 IDELR 197 (W.D. Mo. 2012).

Lathrop R-II School District v. Gray, 611 F.3d 419, 54 IDELR 276 (8th Cir. 2010).

Lee's Summit R-VII School District, 9 ECLRP 86 (SEA Mo. 2012).

Letter to Clarke, 48 IDELR 77 (OSEP 2007).

Letter to Chandler, 59 IDELR 110 (OSEP 2012).

Letter to McKethan, 25 IDELR 295 (OCR 1996).

Letter to Richards, 55 IDELR 107 (OSEP 2010).

Letter to Unnerstall, 68 IDELR 22 (OSEP 2016).

L.H. v. Hamilton County Department of Education, 900 F.3d 779, 72 IDELR 204 (6th Cir. 2018).

Lincoln-Sudbury Regional School District v. Wallis W., 71 IDELR 153 (D. Mass. 2018).

L.J. v. School Board of Broward County Florida, 927 F.3d 1203, 74 IDELR 185 (11th Cir. 2019).

Mamaroneck Union Free School District, 51 IDELR 176 (2nd Cir. 2009).

...Continued

Marshall Joint School District No. 2 v. C.D., 54 IDELR 307 (7th Cir. 2010).

Mesa County Valley School District 51, 68 IDELR 84 (SEA Colo. 2016).

M.G. v. Williamson County Schools, 720 F. App'x 280, 71 IDELR 102 (6th Cir. 2018, unpublished).

Montgomery Township Board of Education, 43 IDELR 186 (3rd Cir. 2005, unpublished).

Mr. and Mrs. M. v. Ridgefield Board of Education, 47 IDELR 258 (D. Conn. 2007).

Mr. I. v. Maine School Administrative District No. 55, 480 F.3d 1, 47 IDELR 121 (1st Cir. 2007).

M.S. v. Mullica Township Board of Education, 49 IDELR 154 (3rd Cir. 2008).

Murray v. Montrose County School District, 51 F.3d 921 (10th Cir. 1995).

North Carolina (NC) Department of Public Instruction, 43 IDELR 229 (OCR 2005).

Palm Beach County School Board, 118 LRP 14832 (SEA Fla. 2017).

Pangerl v. Peoria Unified School District, 780 F. App'x 505, 74 IDELR 246 (9th Cir. 2019, unpublished).

Park v. Anaheim Union High School District, 444 F.3d 1149, 45 IDELR 178 (9th Cir. 2006) (reversed; remanded on other issues, 464 F.3d 1025, 46 IDELR 151 (9th Cir. 2006)).

P.F. v. Stanford Taylor, 119 LRP 1475 (7th Cir. 2018).

PGA Tour Inc. v. Casey Martin, 121 S. Ct. 1879 (US 2001).

Questions and Answers on Endrew F. v. Douglas County School District Re-1, 71 IDELR 68 (US ED 2017).

R.F. v. Cecil County Public Schools, 919 F.3d 237, 74 IDELR 31 (4th Cir. 2019).

...Continued

R.L. v. Miami-Dade County Schools, 757 F.3d 1173, 63 IDELR 182 (11th Cir. 2014).

Roland M. v. Concord School Committee, 910 F.2d 983, 16 IDELR 1129 (1st Cir. 1990).

R.S. v. Board of Directors of Woods Charter School Company, 73 IDELR 252 (M.D. N.C. 2019).

R.Z.C. v. North Shore School District, 755 F. App'x 658, 73 IDELR 139 (9th Cir. 2018, unpublished).

Shelby County (TN) School District, 45 IDELR 259 (OCR 2005).

Sherman and Nishanian v. Mamaroneck Union Free School District, 340 F.3d 87, 39 IDELR 181 (2nd Cir. 2003).

Solorio v. Clovis Unified School District, 748 F. App'x 146, 74 IDELR 2 (9th Cir. 2019, unpublished).

Somoza v. New York City Department of Education, 47 IDELR 127 (S.D. N.Y. 2007).

T.B. and E.B. v. Warwick School Committee, et al., 361 F.3d 80; 40 IDELR 253 (1st Cir. 2004).

Timberlane Regional School District, 45 IDELR 139 (SEA N.H. 2006).

T.S. v. Board of Education of the Town of Ridgefield, 10 F.3d 87, 20 IDELR 889 (2nd Cir. 1993).

Tuscaloosa County Board of Education, 118 LRP 1 (SEA Ala. 2017).

T.W. v. Unified School District #259, 36 F. App'x 122, 43 IDELR 187 (10th Cir. 2005).

Vance County (NC) Schools, 53 IDELR 168 (OCR 2009).

Watson v. Kingston City School District, 142 F. App'x 9, 43 IDELR 244 (2nd Cir. 2005).

Westerville City Schools, 116 LRP 29480 (SEA Ohio 2016).

A SAGE Publishing Company

Helping educators make the greatest impact

CORWIN HAS ONE MISSION: to enhance education through intentional professional learning.

We build long-term relationships with our authors, educators, clients, and associations who partner with us to develop and continuously improve the best evidence-based practices that establish and support lifelong learning.